M000191393

FORGING A PATH OF COMMUNITY & SOCIAL JUSTICE

IN AMERICA

We are living in a time of both turbulence and great promise. Bahá'u'lláh said, *"This is the Day in which God's most excellent favors have been poured out upon men, the Day in which His most mighty grace hath been infused into all created things. It is incumbent upon all the peoples of the world to reconcile their differences, and, with perfect unity and peace, abide beneath the shadow of the Tree of His care and loving-kindness."*

We face challenges unlike any others in history, but we need not succumb to confusion and fear. We have, in the form of the divine teachings of Bahá'u'lláh, guidance that will help us rise to present-day challenges and forge a path toward creating the glorious future that awaits humanity.

"The All-Knowing Physician hath His finger on the pulse of mankind. He perceiveth the disease, and prescribeth, in His unerring wisdom, the remedy. Every age hath its own problem, and every soul its particular aspiration. The remedy the world needeth in its present-day afflictions can never be the same as that which a subsequent age may require. Be anxiously concerned with the needs of the age ye live in, and center your deliberations on its exigencies and requirements."

By first recognizing the truth that we are one humanity and that we now have the capacity to come together, we can arise and create a better world for all.

This publication is dedicated to sharing experiences of those embarking on a path of purposeful action guided by the vision of Bahá'u'lláh. We invite you to engage and find confidence, assurance and hope.

O SON OF SPIRIT! The best beloved of all things in My sight is Justice; turn not away therefrom if thou desirest Me, and neglect it not that I may confide in thee.

— BAHÁ'U'LLÁH

CONTENTS

1.

A SPIRITUAL APPROACH TO

HEALING DIVISIONS

IN AMERICA

The purpose of justice is the appearance of unity among men.

—BAHÁ'U'LLÁH

Bahá'ís and their friends and neighbors from all walks of life are learning to apply profound spiritual principles to gain personal insight and to address social problems they encounter in their own lives and communities in America.

One of these principles is justice. Justice is necessary to bring about unity in diversity. Unifying approaches are necessary to bring about justice.

As they reflect on the positive changes taking place in their own hearts and minds as well as the tangible results they see in their neighborhoods, they become eager to learn more and share what they are learning with others. This path is wide and welcoming for all to advance at their own pace, accompanying and encouraging each other, so that together we might move towards a more advanced society.

Come learn with us!

In an era of rapid, often unsettling change, when society feels increasingly polarized, we look for sensible, empowering and unifying solutions. When environmental, technological and social changes fill us with mixed feelings of restlessness, anxiety and dread, we look for hope and a way toward justice. As our society's capacity for civil discourse becomes frayed, we long to be heard. We seek insight, connectedness and assurance.

All men have been created
to carry forward an ever-
advancing civilization.

— BAHÁ'U'LLÁH

A time of turbulence and transition

The community-building efforts of the Bahá'ís and their friends are based on the belief that humanity is living at a very special time in its history. In its development, humankind has passed through stages similar to infancy and adolescence and now stands at the beginning of its maturity.

This stage of maturity will witness the unification of the human race and the flowering of a diverse, just and peaceful global civilization. Two inseparable processes, one of disintegration and the other of integration, are propelling humanity forward.

The process of disintegration is visible in the violence, war and corruption that go together with the collapse of an outmoded order now incapable of dealing with the needs of a maturing world.

The tensions, divisions and injustices that currently beset America are symptoms of a longstanding illness—a spiritual disorder that shows up in rampant materialism, widespread moral decay and a deeply ingrained racial prejudice.

No one is immune to this disorder—we are all members of this society and to some degree suffer the effects of its maladies. Millions of Americans, subject to systemic injustices in many facets of life, are prevented from both contributing fully to, and from partaking fully of, the benefits of society.

From a Bahá'í perspective, though, there is a promise of healing.

Bahá'ís have long been building diverse American communities such as this one in Kenosha, Wisconsin, 1921.

A vision of the oneness of humanity

A spiritual perspective on the challenges of our day can be found in the writings of Bahá'u'lláh (1817–1892). These divinely-inspired writings are the foundation of the Bahá'í Faith.

Bahá'u'lláh's mission was to educate humanity for its long-awaited coming of age, which will culminate in the era of worldwide justice and peace foretold in sacred scriptures since ancient times. His writings offer a deeply spiritual vision, revolutionary social principles, and practical approaches that will ultimately lead humanity through its stormy adolescence into maturity.

Bahá'u'lláh's teachings center on the principle of oneness—the truth that humanity is one family. Recognition of our oneness has profound implications for both personal behavior and for the way society is organized. Accepting our oneness challenges many current assumptions and revolutionizes our notions of the relationships between the individual, society and its institutions.

When relationships among community members and between them and their institutions are characterized by love and justice, all have the opportunity to use their God-given attributes to advance social good. When spiritual and scientific knowledge is accessible to all and generated through shared experience, a community can learn together to apply it to their collective life. Bahá'ís and those who share this vision are working to advance this process of transformation.

> *We cherish the hope that the light of justice may shine upon the world and sanctify it from tyranny.*
>
> —BAHÁ'U'LLÁH

The Prophet's son visits

In 1912, 'Abdu'l-Bahá, the son of Bahá'u'lláh, the Founder of the Bahá'í Faith, traveled from coast to coast across the continent. While praising the nation's vitality and spirit of enterprise and innovation, He also warned of the dire consequences of failing to remove the stains of ingrained racial prejudices, materialism and political corruption from its civic life. He called on America to become a land of spiritual distinction and leadership and gave a powerful vision of America's spiritual destiny: to lead the way in establishing the oneness of humanity.

'Abdu'l-Bahá offered His vision in a prayer for America:

Confirm this revered nation to upraise the standard of the oneness of humanity, to promulgate the Most Great Peace, to become thereby most glorious and praiseworthy among all the nations of the world. O God! This American nation is worthy of Thy favors and is deserving of Thy mercy. Make it precious and near to Thee through Thy bounty and bestowal.

O People! Consort with the followers of all religions in a spirit of friendliness and fellowship.

— BAHÁ'U'LLÁH

The destiny of America

The Bahá'í writings affirm the special, spiritual role of America in helping the whole human race realize its oneness and establish an age of peace. While the United States was the first nation to be established on the principles that "all men are created equal" and are "endowed by their Creator with certain inalienable rights," its founding was tragically marred by the brutal genocide of American Indian nations, the enslavement of African Americans and the exclusion of women. Subsequent American history may be seen as a struggle to confront and grapple with this legacy. When justice is achieved in this nation, its effects will be global.

The experience of the Bahá'í community

The Bahá'í community recognizes the many challenges it faces as it strives to live up to its own lofty ideals. It is work that will take generations. The Bahá'í community is committed to the long-term process of learning through action. We believe that faith and spirituality have vital and transformative roles in society and the power to release the potential of individuals, communities and institutions.

At the heart of Bahá'í endeavor is a long-term process of social transformation that seeks to develop patterns of life and social structures based on the oneness of humanity. One component is an educational process in which spiritual matters are explored in ways that connect participants with the Word of God while nurturing their commitment to the service of others.

Every soul is invited to contribute regardless of race, class, religion, age or gender. As thousands upon thousands participate in building empowered, diverse communities, they draw insights from both science and the world's spiritual heritage and contribute to the development of new knowledge. Transformation of the individual and transformation of the community unfold simultaneously.

Bahá'ís also engage in various forms of social action, collaborating with others to apply spiritual principles to promote social and economic well-being. They participate in discourse in diverse spheres, as well, from neighborhoods to academic and professional settings, to national and international forums.

In the following pages, we invite you to explore and engage with the Bahá'í model for achieving lasting, positive change. Consider what role you might play in this profound process of personal and social transformation.

Be anxiously concerned with the needs of the age ye live in, and center your deliberations on its exigencies and requirements.

— BAHÁ'U'LLÁH

A SPIRITUAL FRAMEWORK

FOR SOCIAL CHANGE

A NEW TAKE ON RELIGION

The knowledge of such sciences, however, should be acquired as can profit the peoples of the earth, and not those which begin with words and end with words.

— BAHÁ'U'LLÁH

The Bahá'í teachings offer a perspective on religion that may be good news to many people who feel spiritual, but not religious.

What if religion brought people together rather than separating them with exclusivity, judgment and conflicting dogma? What if religion tapped into the innate spiritual powers of each person, creating means to apply spiritual insights to practical social challenges, without rituals or clergy? What if religion were understood as a system of knowledge, parallel to and compatible with science?

Throughout human history, religion at its best has cultivated in whole populations the capacity to love, to give generously, to serve others, to forgive, to trust in God and to sacrifice for the common good. Whole civilizations have been founded upon the moral and spiritual insights that the Divine Educators, spiritual Teachers sent by a loving Creator to guide humanity, have brought to the world.

According to Bahá'í teachings, true religion is a source of unity; true religion is in harmony with science. Without scientific insights and rational thought, religion falls prey to superstition and blind imitation of the past. Without the moral and ethical imperative introduced by religion, science is vulnerable to materialistic forces and can veer toward base and destructive ends.

Bahá'ís believe that religion and science, as two knowledge systems, complement one another in efforts to bring about meaningful social transformation and to address the vexing problems that plague humanity today.

WE NEED

♡VE EACH OTHER

R VIVE.

When I think race..
redlining   oppres
beauty   ~~repression~~
injustice   adversity culture
              institutional diversity
division racism differentea
ID
skapegont   human race
                  ethnicity
environmental   Social constru
racism

CHANNELING
THE POWER OF
THE HUMAN SPIRIT

The fundamental purpose animating the Faith of God and His Religion is to safeguard the interests and promote the unity of the human race, and to foster the spirit of love and fellowship.

— BAHÁ'U'LLÁH

What is a spiritual framework for social change? How is it different from efforts pursued by political parties or educational and advocacy organizations?

For one thing, justice requires universal participation. Social change can't be an effort by one segment of humanity to impose its vision on another, however altruistic the motivation may be. The divisiveness that characterizes current party politics must give way to cooperation. In a society that reflects the principle of the oneness of humankind, we must leave behind a concept of power as a means of domination or superiority, based on contest, contention, division or cultural difference. The Bahá'í framework is intended to release, encourage and channel a different kind of power: the power of the human spirit, the power of unity, of love, of humble service, of pure deeds. From this perspective, power is not a finite entity to be seized and jealously guarded; it constitutes a limitless capacity that resides in the human race as a whole.

The Bahá'í perspective on social change is contextualized by a particular view of history. Humanity is engaged in a long process of social evolution and currently stands on the brink of the next stage of its development: a planet where all inhabitants enjoy spiritual and material prosperity. As human civilization approaches this stage, profound transformation has to occur in both human consciousness at the individual level, and in the structure of social institutions.

Bahá'ís are engaged in civilization-building work—a civilization that no one has ever seen before. Since no one has ever seen such a society, we need to be humble and approach this task with an attitude of learning, starting with small efforts in our own neighborhoods. Clearly, no single group has the answer to humanity's ills, otherwise we would already be living in the world we envision. Together with their neighbors, Bahá'ís set out to learn what contributes to the material and spiritual progress of their neighborhood. They work alongside others to discover together how the Word of God can generate the profound transformation that is required both of the individual and of the structures of society.

The essential elements of the Bahá'í framework include:

one

The oneness of humanity is the fundamental principle of the Bahá'í Faith. It is, in fact, both the goal and the operating principle of the Bahá'í approach to social change. While the spiritual oneness of the human race has been a basic truth ever since the dawn of our existence, we are now at the threshold of an age when this principle can find practical expression.

two

A two-fold moral purpose is at the heart of the Bahá'í model of social change: to refine one's own inner character and to offer service to humanity. Social and personal transformation are inseparable. Being and doing go together. One cannot acquire a spiritual virtue, such as love, patience or generosity without practicing it.

THREE

This framework identifies **three partners** in driving social change:

- **The individual** prays, studies, forms friendships, starts meaningful conversations, initiates acts of service and accompanies others in the learning process.

- **The institutions** channel human and material resources into areas of service, nurture a welcoming environment, work for a spiritual and unified community.

- **The community** builds on a nucleus of friends who pool and coordinate their efforts; it values all perspectives; it celebrates everyone's accomplishments.

four

Four core grassroots activities strengthen participants' spiritual identities and allow them to link their own personal growth to the development of the community. (details in Chapter 4):

- **Devotional gatherings** (all ages)
- **Children's classes** (ages 5–11)
- **Junior youth groups** (ages 12–14)
- **Study circles** (age 15–adult)

A CYCLE OF STUDY, CONSULTATION, ACTION & REFLECTION

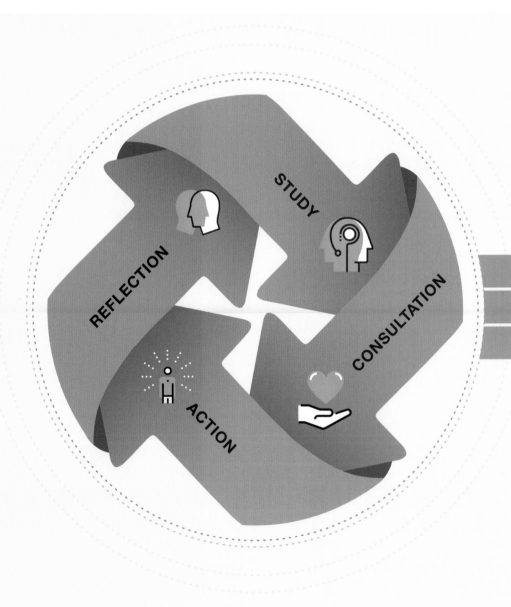

- **Study** of moral and social principles found in the Bahá'í writings

- **Consultation** on resources and opportunities

- **Action** plans devised and carried out

- **Reflection** on outcomes

- **Cycle repeats** to ensure a healthy process of learning in which everyone participates and contributes to knowledge

Bahá'ís and their friends engage in systematic learning involving cycles of **study, consultation, action** and **reflection**. They study moral and social principles found in the Bahá'í writings, consult on and carry out action plans, reflect together on results and repeat the cycle to build a collective body of knowledge.

THREE BROAD AREAS OF ACTIVITY

Building diverse communities: individual and collective empowerment

The main thrust of Bahá'í efforts toward social change is to build vibrant communities characterized by unity in diversity, mutual support and collective well-being. Children, youth and adults engage in their own moral development as they explore spiritual concepts and apply them in their own lives. Women and men alike, from the complete spectrum of racial and ethnic populations, have full partnership in a grassroots process of learning and capacity building.

See Chapter 4

Applying spiritual principles to social and economic life

The Bahá'í framework inspires participants to identify social and material needs and opportunities in their communities and address them through increasingly complex projects and acts of service.

See Chapter 5

Transforming society through discourse

As we learn to apply spiritual principles to our personal, family and community lives, we gain capacity to contribute constructively to ongoing conversations at all levels of society: in neighborhoods, through a diverse array of personal and professional friendships, and in education, advocacy and government settings.

See Chapter 6

*In truth, knowledge is
a veritable treasure for
man, and a source of
glory, of bounty, of joy,
of exultation, of cheer
and gladness unto him.*

—BAHÁ'U'LLÁH

STUDY &
APPLICATION OF
THE WORD
OF GOD

Bahá'ís believe that in every age God reveals His Word through the utterances and writings of His Messengers, the Founders of the world's religions. These words have a creative and transformative effect on the human soul.

Study and meditation on the Word of God, both individually and collectively, releases powerful spiritual and moral forces that find expression in new social relations, revitalized institutions and a vibrant community life. Personal and social transformation begins when deep reflection on the Creative Word is linked with acts of service to humanity.

To systematically enable the participation of ever-larger numbers of people in this process, the Bahá'í community has adopted the "training institute," which functions as a system of distance education. Its principal elements include study circles, tutors and a set of materials grounded in the Bahá'í writings that express the spiritual insights and knowledge gained in translating Bahá'u'lláh's teachings into reality.

THE INSTITUTE PROCESS:
WALKING A SPIRITUAL PATH

The Bahá'í teachings emphasize that each person is responsible for his or her own spiritual development. While Bahá'í institutions offer guidance and support, and the Bahá'í community is a source of love and encouragement, the responsibility for engaging with the Word of God and for spiritual growth ultimately rests with each individual. The Bahá'í institute process facilitates this study and growth.

A person's spiritual journey can be considered as walking a path accompanied by others. It is a path open to all of humanity—a path, Bahá'ís believe, that will allow us to build a better world together. (See pages 38-39 for more on four core community-building activities.)

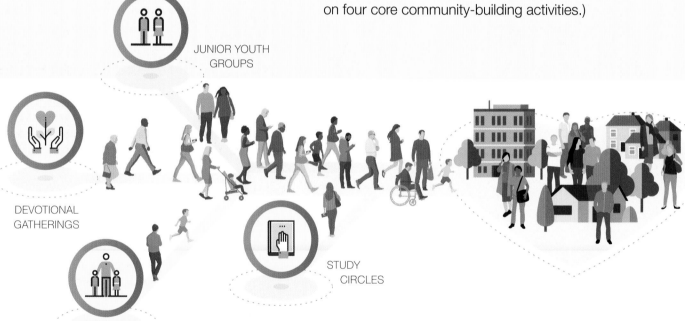

JUNIOR YOUTH GROUPS

DEVOTIONAL GATHERINGS

STUDY CIRCLES

CHILDREN'S CLASSES

Study circles

A study circle is a small group that meets regularly for a few hours, usually in the home of one of its members, to study course materials that include passages from the Bahá'í writings on specific themes. Participants explore: how to create environments that put people in contact with the spiritual forces released through prayer and devotion; how to strengthen bonds of friendship and communicate meaningfully with people of various backgrounds; how to make the education of children an integral part of community life; how to help young people develop their intellectual and spiritual capacities; and how to generate dynamics within the family unit that give rise to material and spiritual prosperity.

In response to the materials they study and with coordinated support, participants carry out specific acts of service. Men and women, young and old alike, come to recognize that they have the power to re-create the world around them. As more people become committed to the vision of transformation fostered by the institute courses, they gradually build a pattern of life that places service and worship at its center.

"The main sequence of courses is organized so as to set the individual, whether Bahá'í or not, on a path being defined by the accumulating experience of the community in its endeavour to open before humanity the vision of Bahá'u'lláh's World Order.

The very notion of a path is, itself, indicative of the nature and purpose of the courses, for a path invites participation,

it beckons to new horizons,

it demands effort and movement,

it accommodates different paces and strides,

it is structured and defined.

A path can be experienced and known, not only by one or two but by scores upon scores; it belongs to the community.

To walk a path is a concept equally expressive.

It requires of the individual volition and choice;

it calls for a set of skills and abilities but also elicits certain qualities and attitudes;

it necessitates a logical progression but admits, when needed, related lines of exploration;

it may seem easy at the outset but becomes more challenging further along.

And crucially, one walks the path in the company of others."

— *The Universal House of Justice*
(international governing council of the Bahá'í Faith)
December 12, 2011

To learn if there is a study circle meeting near you call 1-800-22-UNITE.

A selection of courses from the training institute that focus on building capacity to walk a path of service:

Reflections on the Life of the Spirit
The Creative Word, the nature of prayer and the mystery of life after death

Arising to Serve
The path of service and the essential features of community life

Teaching Children's Classes
The transformative effect of the spiritual education of children

Releasing the Powers of Junior Youth
The spiritual empowerment of adolescents ages 12 to 14

Walking Together on a Path of Service
The training of tutors who assist others to advance through the sequence of courses

Building Vibrant Communities
Accompanying one another on a path of service and consultation

WHERE CAN YOU FIND THE BAHÁ'ÍS?

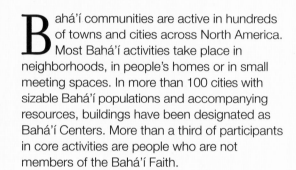

Bahá'í communities are active in hundreds of towns and cities across North America. Most Bahá'í activities take place in neighborhoods, in people's homes or in small meeting spaces. In more than 100 cities with sizable Bahá'í populations and accompanying resources, buildings have been designated as Bahá'í Centers. More than a third of participants in core activities are people who are not members of the Bahá'í Faith.

Blessed is the spot, and the house, and the place, and the city, and the heart, and the mountain, and the refuge, and the cave, and the valley, and the land, and the sea, and the island, and the meadow where mention of God hath been made, and His praise glorified.

—BAHÁ'U'LLÁH

There is one continental Bahá'í House of Worship in the United States, in Wilmette, Illinois, just north of Chicago. This sacred space is open to all people as a haven for personal prayer and contemplation. The central purpose of Bahá'í Temples is to join worship and service—in other words, to put prayer into action through service to others. There are no clergy, sermons or rituals.

Bahá'í institutions operate three year-round conference and retreat centers—in California, Michigan and Maine—that offer a wide range of programming for adults, youth and children. In addition, the Native American Bahá'í Institute serves the Navajo Nation in northern Arizona. Seasonal schools are held during winter and summer breaks at community centers, college campuses and other locations around the country. Generally lasting a few days to a week, these programs offer informal, family-friendly spaces where people can deepen friendships and learn more about the Bahá'í Faith.

 To connect with Bahá'ís near you, call 1-800-22-UNITE or go to www.bahai.us/contact

Gather ye together with the utmost joy and fellowship and recite the verses revealed by the merciful Lord. By so doing the doors to true knowledge will be opened to your inner beings, and ye will then feel your souls endowed with steadfastness and your hearts filled with radiant joy.

—BAHÁ'U'LLÁH

THE IMPORTANCE OF THE ARTS IN THE BAHÁ'Í FAITH

The pursuit of the arts—drama, poetry and other forms of written expression, instrumental music and song, and visual art such as painting, architecture and crafts—are all expressly encouraged in the Bahá'í writings. The arts serve both as channels of personal and communal expression and as forms of learning and exploration of reality. They uplift hearts, connect people and mirror the qualities of God.

In this wonderful new age, art is worship. The more thou strivest to perfect it, the closer wilt thou come to God. What bestowal could be greater than this, that one's art should be even as the act of worshipping the Lord?

— 'ABDU'L-BAHÁ

"*It is natural for the heart and spirit to take pleasure and enjoyment in all things that show forth symmetry, harmony, and perfection,*" 'Abdu'l-Bahá said. "*For instance: a beautiful house, a well-designed garden, a symmetrical line, a graceful motion, a well written book, pleasing garments—in fact, all things that have in themselves grace or beauty are pleasing to the heart and spirit.*"

Acts of artistic expression are equated with worship, drawing people nearer to God. Music, crafts and other arts are considered of the utmost importance, from childhood on, and diverse artistic endeavors are essential to community life.

"*All Art is a gift of the Holy Spirit,*" 'Abdu'l-Bahá said. "*When this light shines through the mind of a musician, it manifests itself in beautiful harmonies. Again, shining through the mind of a poet, it is seen in fine poetry and poetic prose. When the Light of the Sun of Truth inspires the mind of a painter, he produces marvellous pictures. These gifts are fulfilling their highest purpose, when showing forth the praise of God.*"

THE BAHÁ'Í FAITH AT A GLANCE

ONE God

Called by different names throughout the ages, the eternal God, the Creator of the universe, is limitless, all-knowing, all-powerful and all-loving. God is one. While the reality of God is beyond human understanding, we may find expressions of God's attributes in every created thing.

The peoples of the world, of whatever race or religion, derive their inspiration from one heavenly Source, and are the subjects of one God.

— BAHÁ'U'LLÁH

ONE Human Family

Beyond all differences of race, culture, class or ethnicity, regardless of differences in customs, opinions, or temperaments, every individual is a member of one gloriously diverse human family. Each unique individual has a role to play in carrying forward an ever-advancing material and spiritual civilization.

Ye are the fruits of one tree, and the leaves of one branch. Deal ye one with another with the utmost love and harmony, with friendliness and fellowship.

— BAHÁ'U'LLÁH

ONE Unfolding Religion

Humanity's spiritual, intellectual and moral capacities have been cultivated through the successive teachings of the Founders of the world's religions—the Manifestations of God. Among Them are Krishna, Abraham, Moses, Zoroaster, Buddha, Jesus Christ, Muhammad and, most recently, the Báb and Bahá'u'lláh. Each religion originates with God and is suited to the age and place in which it is revealed. In essence, the religion of God is one and is progressively unfolding.

This is the changeless Faith of God, eternal in the past, eternal in the future.

— BAHÁ'U'LLÁH

PROGRESSIVE REVELATION

The Revelation of God may be likened to the sun. No matter how innumerable its risings, there is but one sun, and upon it depends the life of all things.

—THE BÁB

KRISHNA

ABRAHAM

MOSES

ZOROASTER

BUDDH

5,000
YEARS AGO

4,000
YEARS AGO

3,000
YEARS AGO

True religion, like science, advances and evolves over time. From a Bahá'í perspective, evolution and renewal of religion occurs with the coming of a new Manifestation of God, sometimes called a Divine Educator or Messenger of God, approximately every 500 to 1,000 years. This process, by which God continuously provides the guidance necessary for humanity's social and spiritual evolution, is known as "progressive revelation."

Each Messenger restates essential and universal spiritual truths, while providing additional guidance suited to the needs of humanity at the time. In this era of global challenges, the teachings of Bahá'u'lláh, the most recent Messenger of God, have the power to spiritually re-awaken and unite the peoples of the world. Bahá'u'lláh's teachings contain the spiritual principles that will guide humanity to create justice and a universal, lasting peace—the great peace that has been promised by all the previous Manifestations of God.

Through their appearance the Revelation of God is made manifest, and by their countenance the Beauty of God is revealed. Thus it is that the accents of God Himself have been heard uttered by these Manifestations of the Divine Being.

—BAHÁ'U'LLÁH

MUHAMMAD

JESUS CHRIST

BAHÁ'U'LLÁH

THE BÁB

2,000
YEARS AGO

1,000
YEARS AGO

TODAY

ABOUT
THE BAHÁ'Í FAITH

Origins

The Bahá'í Faith was born in Persia (today Iran) in the mid-1800s. In less than 200 years it has become a universal faith. Its members come from virtually every national, ethnic, religious and tribal background.

Founders

The Bahá'í Faith originated with **Bahá'u'lláh** (1817–1892), Whose title means "the Glory of God." Bahá'ís regard Him as the latest in the succession of Divine Messengers Who founded the world's major religions. In His writings, Bahá'u'lláh outlines a framework for the development of a global civilization which takes into account both the spiritual and material dimensions of human life. His teachings, centered around the recognition of the oneness of humanity, offer a compelling vision of an approaching world united in justice, peace and prosperity.

Bahá'u'lláh's coming was heralded by the **Báb** (1819–1850), meaning "the Gate." The Báb proclaimed His divine mission in 1844, which is considered the beginning of the Bahá'í Era—a new cycle of human history and social evolution.

A movement of personal and social transformation

The millions of people worldwide who constitute the international Bahá'í community are quite possibly the most diverse organized body on the planet. United by their belief in Bahá'u'lláh, and inspired by His teachings, members strive to live out the twofold moral purpose of transforming their own characters while contributing to the advancement of society.

Sacred writings

The writings of the Báb and Bahá'u'lláh are considered by Bahá'ís to have been revealed by God. As the Creative Word of God, these sacred writings have the power to touch the deepest recesses of our hearts and transform us and the world around us. The Bahá'í writings address the needs of the age and offer inspiration for individuals working to better themselves and their communities. Bahá'u'lláh enjoined His followers to read daily from the sacred texts: *"Immerse yourselves in the ocean of My words, that ye may unravel its secrets, and discover all the pearls of wisdom that lie hid in its depths."*

Worship

Daily prayer, offered both in private and in the company of others, is regarded by Bahá'ís as essential spiritual nourishment, providing inspiration for positive personal and social change. Bahá'ís consider work done in the spirit of service to humanity as the highest form of worship. Individuals pray daily and each spring observe a 19-day period of fasting during daylight hours. The Bahá'í Faith has no clergy or sacraments, and has simple practices for life passages, such as weddings and memorials.

Organization

The affairs of the Bahá'í community are governed by institutions established by Bahá'u'lláh. This Administrative Order comprises both elected and appointed institutions at local, national and international levels. Nonpartisan elections, without nominations or campaigns and conducted by secret ballot, and collective decision making are hallmarks of Bahá'í administration. These and other principles constitute a model of just and unified global governance.

Illuminated Tablet of Bahá'u'lláh. His writings have been translated into more than 800 languages.

God's purpose is none other than to usher in the Golden Age of a long-divided, a long-afflicted humanity. Its present state is distressingly dark. Its distant future, however, is gloriously radiant — so radiant that no eye can visualize it.

— SHOGHI EFFENDI, GUARDIAN OF THE BAHÁ'Í FAITH

Bahá'í House of Worship
for North America, Wilmette, Illinois

A new life is, in this age, stirring within all the peoples of the earth.

—BAHÁ'U'LLÁH

BASIC

TEACHINGS

Bahá'u'lláh's teachings offer hope to a troubled world. He identified the spiritual principles on which humanity may, with divine assistance, establish lasting peace:

- The oneness of humanity
- Independent investigation of truth
- Elimination of prejudice
- Racial and social justice
- The nobility of each human being
- Equality of women and men
- Harmony between science and religion
- Universal education
- Spiritually guided solutions to economic inequality
- Justice and equity as foundations for world peace

Do I have to become a member to take part in Bahá'í activities?

Everyone, regardless of faith or background, is welcome to take part in most Bahá'í activities. Some people, after a period of personal study and reflection, are moved to recognize Bahá'u'lláh as God's Messenger for this day and may choose to formally enroll in the Faith.

How are these activities funded?

Only enrolled members may give to the Bahá'í funds, participate in Bahá'í elections, and serve on local, national and international Bahá'í institutions. Individual Bahá'ís strive to give selflessly and joyfully to the various funds of the Faith. Contributions are private and voluntary, and soliciting money from individuals is not permitted. Voluntary giving fosters an awareness that managing one's financial affairs in accordance with spiritual principles is part of a coherently lived life.

We must be like the fountain or spring that is continually emptying itself of all that it has and is continually being refilled from an invisible source.

– BAHÁ'Í WRITINGS

A SELECTION OF BAHÁ'Í

SACRED WRITINGS

ON HUMAN NATURE

Bahá'u'lláh affirmed that each human being possesses a distinct, rational soul that constitutes the real self. The soul is created in the image and likeness of God, meaning that it is capable of acquiring divine qualities and heavenly attributes.

Understanding the spiritual dimension of human beings must inform all our work toward unity and social justice. The following selections from the Writings of Bahá'u'lláh help us to gradually align our thoughts and behavior to this core reality and, in turn, develop new capacities for meaningful action.

GEMS OF DIVINE MYSTERIES

BAHÁ'Í

THE PROCLAMATION OF BAHÁ'U'LLÁH

BAHÁ'Í

THE SUMMONS OF THE LORD OF HOSTS

BAHÁ'Í

TABLETS OF BAHÁ'U'LLÁH

BAHÁ'Í

BAHÁ'U'LLÁH

THE KITÁB-I-AQDAS

BAHÁ'Í

Bahá'u'lláh

EPISTLE TO THE SON OF THE WOLF

BAHÁ'Í®

Bahá'u'lláh

KITÁB-I-ÍQÁN THE BOOK OF CERTITUDE

BAHÁ'Í®

GLEANINGS FROM THE WRITINGS OF BAHÁ'U'LLÁH

Bahá'í PUBLISHING

PRAYERS AND MEDITATIONS

BAHÁ'U'LLÁH

Bahá'í PUBLISHING

Thou art My dominion and My dominion perisheth not; wherefore fearest thou thy perishing? Thou art My light and My light shall never be extinguished; why dost thou dread extinction? Thou art My glory and My glory fadeth not; thou art My robe and My robe shall never be outworn. Abide then in thy love for Me, that thou mayest find Me in the realm of glory.

Noble have I created thee, yet thou hast abased thyself. Rise then unto that for which thou wast created.

Veiled in My immemorial being and in the ancient eternity of My essence, **I knew My love for thee; therefore I created thee,** *have engraved on thee Mine image and revealed to thee My beauty.*

SELECTIONS FROM THE WRITINGS OF BAHÁ'U'LLÁH

Know ye not why We created you all from the same dust?

That no one should exalt himself over the other. Ponder at all times in your hearts how ye were created. Since We have created you all from one same substance it is incumbent on you to be even as one soul, to walk with the same feet, eat with the same mouth and dwell in the same land, that from your inmost being, by your deeds and actions, the signs of oneness and the essence of detachment may be made manifest. Such is My counsel to you, O concourse of light! **Heed ye this counsel that ye may obtain the fruit of holiness from the tree of wondrous glory.**

Lay not on any soul a load which ye would not wish to be laid upon you, and desire not for anyone the things ye would not desire for yourselves.

I loved thy creation, hence I created thee. Wherefore, do thou love Me, that I may name thy name and fill thy soul with the spirit of life.

Know thou of a truth that the soul, after its separation from the body, will continue to progress until it attaineth the presence of God, in a state and condition which neither the revolution of ages and centuries, nor the changes and chances of this world, can alter. It will endure as long as the Kingdom of God, His sovereignty, His dominion and power will endure. It will manifest the signs of God and His attributes, and will reveal His loving kindness and bounty.

UPON *the inmost reality of each and every created thing He hath shed the light of one of His names, and made it a recipient of the glory of one of His attributes. Upon the reality of man, however, He hath focused the radiance of all of His names and attributes, and made it a mirror of His own Self. Alone of all created things man hath been singled out for so great a favor, so enduring a bounty.*

The purpose of God in creating man hath been, and will ever be, to enable him to know his Creator and to attain His Presence.

These energies with which the Daystar of Divine bounty and Source of heavenly guidance hath endowed the reality of man lie, however, latent within him.... **unless the dross is blotted out from the face of the mirror it can never represent the image of the sun nor reflect its light and glory.**

Having created the world and all that liveth and moveth therein, He, through the direct operation of His unconstrained and sovereign Will, chose to confer upon man the unique distinction and capacity to know Him and to love Him—a capacity that must needs be regarded as the generating impulse and the primary purpose underlying the whole of creation.

BUILDING DIVERSE
COMMUNITIES:
INDIVIDUAL AND
COLLECTIVE EMPOWERMENT

Cleave unto that which draweth you together and uniteth you.

– BAHÁ'U'LLÁH

Bahá'ís consider it a duty to help humanity to come together as one family. The spiritual teachings of the Bahá'í Faith inspire us to reach out across ethnic and class barriers to form deep and diverse relationships and to build communities that nurture the well-being of all people.

The tools Bahá'ís and their friends and neighbors use to build this distinctive community life seem deceptively simple. They are, in reality, profound and revolutionary. There are at present four core activities, all of which have spiritual underpinnings. They create space and opportunity for people to have important, meaningful—and sometimes challenging—conversations that can lead to reconciliation and growth.

When systematically pursued, these activities have the power to create genuine, lasting connections between people. As authentic friendships are forged, underlying community needs can be identified and addressed. In aggregate, they offer whole populations settings in which to begin to undo prejudice and actively strive to overcome racist patterns of thought and behavior.

FOUR CORE ACTIVITIES

TO BUILD A **DISTINCTIVE** COMMUNITY LIFE

1. Devotional gatherings

(all ages) bring people of all backgrounds and beliefs together in prayer and stimulate meaningful conversations that can lead to action. As worship is linked with acts of service, a unifying spirit begins to permeate the community. Gatherings are held in homes or community centers and consist largely of sharing prayers and passages from holy scriptures in an informal, yet respectful, atmosphere.

2. Children's classes

(ages 5–11) provide the early seeds of moral and spiritual education and introduce the idea of equality of all people at an early age. All of the community's children are welcome. These classes help children discover and strengthen their inherent spiritual qualities like kindness, patience and generosity through stories, songs, prayers and art.

3. Junior youth groups

(ages 12–14) motivate young people to explore complex issues, consult about neighborhood needs, plan and carry out acts of service and find positive avenues for recreation and artistic expression. Working with mentors called "animators," youth from all backgrounds develop a global identity, wisdom, compassion, decision-making skills and a mindset of service to others.

4. Study circles

(ages 15–adult) are small groups that meet regularly, usually in the home of a group member, to study passages from the Bahá'í writings on the life of the soul and such themes as learning about consultation, accompanying one another in service and promoting the arts. This training builds capacity, skills and knowledge for a life of service to the community. Participants come to recognize that they have the power to re-create the world around them.

Do not be content with showing friendship in words alone, let your heart burn with loving kindness for all who may cross your path.

—'ABDU'L-BAHÁ

A RICH TAPESTRY
VIDEO SERIES

This series of video stories illustrates how love is being translated into action to address questions of race and culture in the United States.

Watch at www.bahai.us/collection/a-rich-tapestry

COMMUNITY BUILDING STARTS WITH AN ELEVATED CONVERSATION AMONG A FEW PEOPLE

Being Heard in the Face of Paternalism

This story from the Navajo Nation expresses the challenges of one community's journey to overcome a history of mistreatments and paternalistic attitudes. How do we move together from a narrative of oppression to a narrative of oneness? Here is a critical look through the lens of some members of this American Indian culture who are applying the teachings of Bahá'u'll'áh to build a community devoid of prejudice.

Minneapolis: Playing a Humble Part

The Minneapolis Bahá'í Center is a block away from the spot where George Floyd was killed in May 2020. When surrounding streets were shut down for weeks due to protests, the center set up an improvised food pantry. Since then, Bahá'ís have been strengthening connections with the local community through shared acts of service.

COMMUNITY MEMBERS LEARN AND GROW AS THEY SERVE TOGETHER AND ENCOURAGE EACH OTHER

Finding Purpose and a Path of Service

We all like to think we have common sense. But what we think we know gets challenged when we interact with people of different cultures and walks of life. Here is a story of how one young woman is being guided along paths of service in diverse settings as she embraces the Bahá'í Faith.

Prayerful Voices for Change

Inspired by the power of prayer, women in the community of Del Sur, San Diego, transform their words into action and bridge ethnic and cultural divides in their community by starting children's classes, devotional gatherings and study circles.

Building Trust and Community

Chicago's Bronzeville community, a neighborhood with a rich, African American cultural history, struggles with grinding poverty and encroaching gentrification. Here is a story about one resident, a 21-year-old college student, whose trust and openness lead him to assist his Bahá'í neighbors with a weekly children's class.

MEANINGFUL CONVERSATIONS LEAD TO TRUE FRIENDSHIPS ACROSS LINES OF RACE AND CULTURE

It's all about service

Lewiston, Maine, a struggling mill town with a declining population, has seen an influx of immigrants from various African countries. By participating in the junior youth spiritual empowerment program, young immigrants embrace and build on cultural differences while serving their community.

Refresh and Gladden My Spirit

Two mothers in Prince George's County, Maryland, bond through prayer and go on to build a relationship of service that impacts their families and neighbors.

Crossing Ethnic Boundaries

"How are we doing in terms of racial diversity?" This seemingly simple question has inspired new friendships among Mexican American families and their African immigrant neighbors in a Phoenix, Arizona, neighborhood. The result: regular classes for children and teens and a family camp where youth from both communities help their parents begin to overcome racial biases by recognizing shared values and appreciating cultural differences

SOCIAL ACTION: APPLYING SPIRITUAL PRINCIPLES

TO SOCIAL AND ECONOMIC LIFE

While social action may involve the provision of goods and services in some form, its primary concern must be to build capacity within a given population to participate in creating a better world.

—THE UNIVERSAL HOUSE OF JUSTICE
(INTERNATIONAL GOVERNING COUNCIL OF THE BAHÁ'Í FAITH)

Bahá'ís use the term "social action" to refer to a spectrum of endeavors that aim to apply spiritual insights from the teachings of Bahá'u'lláh to improving some aspect of the social or economic life of a population. A group of middle schoolers, for example, may wish to offer a service to their community that is as straightforward as picking up neighborhood trash. Other projects may require a greater degree of complexity. In some instances, full-fledged organizations emerge to address a particular need.

Fundamentally, Bahá'ís believe that every member of the human family has the right, as the noble soul that they are, to benefit from a prosperous world, and each person also has the responsibility to contribute towards the construction of such a world. The way forward is found by encouraging a growing number of people to participate in a collective learning process. Only as we approximate universal participation in this enterprise can we hope for true success.

This approach completely recasts the relationships that should underpin how society operates and how individuals relate to one another and to the whole.

Walk to
End Racism
Wilmette,
Illinois

Just as the cells and organs in the human body are diverse yet all work in harmony for the benefit of the body, so should each individual and population work for the benefit of the whole human race.

Extending the analogy, it would be senseless for the cells of the stomach to consider themselves superior to the cells of the lungs, or vice versa. If that were the case, the body would be doomed to fail. In the same way, there is no room for feelings of superiority, prejudice or paternalism in the work associated with social action.

Bahá'ís and their friends are, of course, not perfect, but they are guided by the pivotal principle of the oneness of humanity when they turn to the writings of Bahá'u'lláh: "O children of men! Know ye not why We created you from the same dust? That no one should exalt himself over the other."

Social action toward racial justice

Particularly in the United States, few challenges are more dire than that of deeply rooted prejudice and racial inequity. As increasing numbers commit themselves to the vision of justice and unity found in the Bahá'í teachings, they begin to see themselves as protagonists in creating lasting change in their home communities. All people share the right to a dignified existence and the responsibility to selflessly contribute their talents and abilities to the creation of a better world.

We can see glimpses of that better world when historically oppressed populations draw on the teachings of Bahá'u'lláh to begin to shed the age-old shackles that continue to be imposed upon them. As the following stories illustrate, some American Indian, African American and recent immigrant populations are making efforts to address oppression by illuminating their everyday individual and collective actions with the Word of God. Stirrings of social action that emerge from this process are often subtle, knowledge-centered and localized.

Navajo Nation

Phoenix

Navajo Nation

At the Native American Bahá'í Institute in the Navajo Nation, participants in the junior youth spiritual empowerment program decided to gather from elders elements of their cultural heritage that are at risk of being forgotten, such as knowledge of native plants and animals, artistic expressions like silversmithing, and spiritual concepts that have lost modern meaning, such as the concept of the beauty way— living in a way that is spiritual, profound and pleasing to the Creator.

As the youth engaged elders in conversations they became aware of some of the community's material needs and devised practical projects to address them. Some of these include initiating a clothing drive, distributing school supplies, helping the elderly with home maintenance, picking up litter by the highway, repairing potholes in the road, mending fences and caring for livestock. Two of the junior youths' projects (a food drive and hauling wood) have evolved into annual mainstays of the community.

Phoenix, Arizona

The Creighton neighborhood of Phoenix is comprised of immigrants, mostly of Hispanic and African origin. Parents engage in Bahá'í study circles and host devotional gatherings that rotate among a growing group of families. Joining families together in devotions has led to conversations about alcoholism among fathers and youth, consultation on how to collectively navigate challenges with the school system and college applications, and a workshop on nutrition and wellness in the neighborhood.

The transformative power of thousands upon thousands of simple actions undertaken at the grassroots tied together in a common framework should not be underestimated.

— BAHÁ'Í OFFICE OF SOCIAL AND ECONOMIC DEVELOPMENT

Durham

Florence

Listeners in a largely rural area of northeast South Carolina relied on Radio Bahá'í WLGI 90.9 FM in Hemingway for up-to-date reports on weather, roads and power outages during 2018's Hurricane Florence. The station's regular programming of spiritually uplifting songs and public service information is intended to contribute to positive social change in the 75-mile radius it serves.

Durham, North Carolina

Local youth are eagerly seizing the opportunity to serve the historically African-American neighborhood of central Durham, located near North Carolina Central University. Young members of this historically oppressed population are finding pride in and ownership of their community's destiny.

Florence, South Carolina

The culture of sharing intergenerational knowledge found in the African-American population of Florence is enhancing the social fabric of those involved in the community building work. Some 20-30 African-American youth participate in bi-weekly gatherings focused on lively devotions, music and discussion of issues that assail them on a daily basis. The institute process is an integral part of the youths' experience with intensive study every Sunday.

Chelsea

Farmville

Memphis

For more stories about contributing to social and material progress, see **www.bahai.us/tag/social-action/**

Farmville, Virginia

A local community center serves as a hub for a range of activities illumined by contact with the Word of God. The Mom's Devotional Gathering hosted there is not just a space for prayer and uplifting fellowship, but is also an environment where practical support emerges for the predominantly African-American population in one of the country's "whitest cities."

Memphis, Tennessee

The community-building efforts surged forward when an African-American youth returned to his hometown and devoted his energies to promoting Bahá'u'lláh's vision for humanity. As he shared that vision with neighbors, family members and students at his former high school, some of them discovered that they have a role in advancing it. At the same time, he is working alongside fellow Bahá'ís in western Tennessee as they gain the confidence to talk with neighbors about serving their community and to provide paths for that service. In all this, he is drawing on experience he gained as a participant in a South Carolina initiative that enables young Bahá'ís, especially African

Americans, to move to towns and neighborhoods where that kind of activity is intensive.

Chelsea, Massachusetts

In one infamously divided (predominantly Hispanic) neighborhood of Boston, a hopeful vision of spiritual and social transformation is emerging from a culturally diverse group of young friends.

Most appropriately conceived in terms of a spectrum, social action can range from fairly informal efforts of limited duration undertaken by individuals or small groups of friends to programmes of social and economic development with a high level of complexity and sophistication implemented by Bahá'í-inspired organizations. Irrespective of its scope and scale, all social action seeks to apply the teachings and principles of the Faith to improve some aspect of the social or economic life of a population, however modestly.

— UNIVERSAL HOUSE OF JUSTICE
(INTERNATIONAL GOVERNING COUNCIL OF THE BAHÁ'Í FAITH)

ENGAGING IN DISCOURSE:
TRANSFORMING SOCIETY AT THE
LEVEL OF THOUGHT

The well-being of mankind, its peace and security are unattainable unless and until its unity is firmly established.

— BAHÁ'U'LLÁH

Working toward unity and social justice requires changing not only individual and collective behaviors and attitudes, but also social structures and institutions. Transformation at both of these levels begins with reshaping the intellectual foundations that underpin existing behaviors and structures. In other words, society needs to change at the level of thought. This is the focus of the Bahá'í community's efforts to engage in public discourse.

Recognition of the principle of the oneness of humankind necessitates the abandonment of prejudice of every kind—race, class, color, gender, creed, nationality, age, material wealth—everything that people have used to consider themselves superior or inferior to others. From this perspective, unity is seen as the essential starting point, rather than as a distant goal that would be achieved only after battling societal ills and injustices one by one.

By exploring concepts such as these in ongoing conversations at all levels of society, we can assist our fellow citizens to unite on the basis of commonly held ideals and principles and work together for a social order free of prejudice and characterized by unity in diversity. Some meaningful conversations come about naturally in the course of neighborhood community building, as well as through diverse friendships and personal and professional connections. Other conversations occur in a variety of social spaces, such as conferences and seminars, involving educational, advocacy and governmental agencies.

In such settings, fundamental assumptions can be questioned and alternatives considered. Is human nature inherently selfish? Are there alternatives to competition as a framework for progress? What is the nature of "freedom"? How can diversity and inclusion strengthen a given structure?

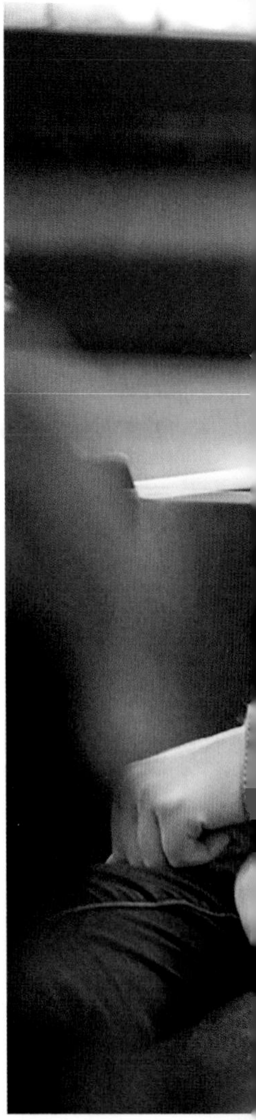

AT EVERY LEVEL

WE HAVE MUCH TO LEARN

Contributing to the national discourse on race

To learn ever-more deeply about bringing Bahá'í ideals of unity and justice into the national conversation on race, a team of race discourse officers has been working for several years within the Bahá'í Office of Public Affairs in Washington, D.C. They participate in a range of social spaces where racism is discussed, building relationships with a wide variety of people.

Participants consult in a Faith and Race Dialogue in September 2018. The United States Bahá'í Office of Public Affairs organizes these gatherings to explore the role faith plays in overcoming ingrained prejudice and structural injustice in the country.

"Walking Together on a Path Toward Race Amity" programs build capacity for meaningful conversations at the neighborhood level

After more than a year's consultation, reflection and testing, a fledgling program on "Walking Together on a Path Toward Race Amity" was introduced in May through September 2019 at three Bahá'í retreat centers and more than 20 weekend seasonal schools.

Compiled by a multiethnic task force, the study materials include excerpts from Bahá'í guidance. Two brief case studies, one looking at the impact of racism on families and the other examining a conflict in a junior youth group, are followed by

questions for discussion. Where possible, smaller study groups include two or more generations within families or neighborhoods. They practice conversations such as those they might have on visits to each other's homes. A number of the groups started putting together action plans on the spot—plans to work beyond racial and ethnic barriers as they expand circles of friends who pray, converse, study and build capacities together.

Nanjira Sambuli (left), a Kenyan digital-equality advocate, speaks with audience members after presenting at the Bahá'í Chair's Future of Humanity Conference.

The Chair's 2018 Annual Lecture featured Jabari Mahiri, Professor of Education at the University of California, Berkeley, whose research re-examines the unscientific basis of "race" as a construct.

"Searching for solutions to intractable social problems that are barriers to peace is the highest aim of the Bahá'í Chair," says Hoda Mahmoudi, the professor serving as its director, here with Dr. Rashawn Ray of the University of Maryland.

Bahá'í Chair for World Peace series on structural racism

Every academic year since 2012, the Bahá'í Chair for World Peace at the University of Maryland has hosted an extraordinary series of programs and events exploring structural racism and the root causes of prejudice. The series has featured close to 30 of the leading national and international scholars who explore pathways to the elimination of racial prejudice. The lectures are well attended by students, faculty and staff, and are also open and free to the public.

The Bahá'í Chair is an endowed academic program that advances interdisciplinary examination and discourse on global peace. Established in 1993, the Chair promotes the vision for world peace through an intensive learning process focused on five central themes: structural racism, human nature, the empowerment of women, global governance and the globalization of environmental challenges.

Douglas White, a lawyer and negotiator who serves Native peoples of Canada, shares his own moving stories of struggle growing up on a reservation and becoming a tribal leader and lawyer. He tells how his viewpoint shifted from confrontation to cooperation when he encountered the Bahá'í teachings in pursuit of justice for First Nations peoples. (2019)

Social justice, resilience and action are the focus of Association for Bahá'í Studies annual conferences

The Association for Bahá'í Studies–North America focuses on developing capacity among people of all backgrounds to draw from the Bahá'í teachings to contribute to professional and academic discourses in their respective fields.

The Association's annual conferences go beyond theory to the discussion of the actual work of advancing civilization, using presentations, panels and small breakout groups to examine and question underlying intellectual foundations of discourses impacting social justice.

Henry Box Brown in Flint

In a persuasive example of how the arts can facilitate discourse, audiences of *Henry Box Brown* are invited into conversation and are challenged to pledge to act for social good. The play tells the story of a 33-year-old enslaved person in Virginia who, in 1849, escaped to freedom by mailing himself in a wooden crate to abolitionists in Philadelphia. Plans are underway for nationwide performances by the Children's Theater Company of New York, founded by members of the Bahá'í Faith.

(Left) The Race Amity Leadership Academy offers opportunities for high school students that center on the values of close cross-racial and cross-cultural relationships through field trips, service activities and scholarship-supported attendance at the National Race Amity Conference.

(Below) William H. "Smitty" Smith, NCRA Founding Executive Director

National Center for Race Amity

The National Center for Race Amity (NCRA), established in Boston in January 2010, centers its educational and advocacy activities on the conviction that race relations in America will not substantially improve unless the public discourse on race moves beyond a blame-grievance-rejection framework to one that recognizes and celebrates our ability to overcome racial prejudice through association, amity and collaboration.

There is a precedent to this approach. Parallel to our country's history of racial oppression, a largely hidden and poorly understood "other tradition" of close collaboration, amity and love has served as the moral and spiritual counterweight to the dominant portrayal of racism that occupies much of our national history. The NCRA produced the film *An American Story: Race Amity and the Other Tradition* and promotes screenings and discussion groups to foster this hopeful and transformative approach to race relations in America.

For more stories about contributing to public discourse, see **www.bahai.us/tag/public-discourse**

TRACING A
PATH TOWARD UNITY:

1844 TO THE PRESENT

For more than a century, the American Bahá'í community has striven to give expression to the oneness of humanity, the core principle of Bahá'u'lláh's message, by seeking to recognize and eliminate racial prejudice and oppression, advancing the equality of women and men, and deliberately building vibrant spiritual communities that reflect and embrace the human family in all its diversity.

The Bahá'í community's commitment to the principle of the oneness of humanity has offered both inspiration and safe haven to those experiencing fear and oppression in a society divided by the historical influence of slavery and anti-Blackness. It is also a testing ground for others to confront destructive, society-wide notions of white supremacy and the corresponding personal sense of superiority.

Through the years, the community's achievements have shifted from the work of individuals to group efforts and collective advancement. Bahá'ís acknowledge that this journey to oneness is in its earliest stages. The Bahá'í community is a work in progress, fueled by systematic action, hope and the divine promise of Bahá'u'lláh.

‘Abdu’l-Bahá (center) with early Bahá’ís in Chicago’s Lincoln Park in 1912. During His coast-to-coast travels, He tirelessly shared Bahá’u’lláh’s message of unity and loving-kindness and called upon America to become a land of spiritual distinction.

1844

A new cycle of human history and social evolution begins when the Báb declares His mission to prepare humanity for the coming of Bahá'u'lláh, Founder of the Bahá'í Faith.

1863

Bahá'u'lláh publicly declares His mission in Baghdad, Iraq, that the time has come for humanity to recognize its oneness and establish its unity. The new Faith spreads quickly, reaching America by the 1890s.

THE FIRST PUBLIC MENTION OF THE BAHÁ'Í FAITH IN AMERICA

1893

The 1893 Parliament of the World's Religions meets at the Art Institute of Chicago

That all nations should become one in faith and all men as brothers; that the bonds of affection and unity between the sons of men should be strengthened; that diversity of religions should cease and differences of race be annulled. What harm is there in this? Yet so it shall be. These fruitless strifes, these ruinous wars shall pass away, and the 'Most Great Peace' shall come. Do not you in Europe need this also? Let not a man glory in this, that he loves his country; let him rather glory in this, that he loves his kind.

— A QUOTE OF BAHÁ'U'LLÁH READ AT THE WORLD PARLIAMENT OF RELIGIONS

FIRSTS OF THE FAITH

1898

Robert Turner, of California, becomes the first African American Bahá'í.

US enslavement of Africans (1619 – 1865)

American Civil War (1861 – 1865)

1844   1863   1878   1895

Mass expansion of convict leasing (1865 – 1941)

Post-Civil War Reconstruction (1865 – 1877)   Jim Crow, Black Codes, Pig Laws, & Separate But Equal (1877 -

| FOUNDATIONS OF THE BAHÁ'Í FAITH | FIRSTS OF THE FAITH | SOCIAL ACTION OF THE BAHÁ'Í FAITH |

1894

Thornton Chase, of Massachusetts, a white man who commanded a company of Black infantry during the Civil War, becomes the first American Bahá'í. The same year, Kate Ives, from Boston, becomes the first American woman to join the Faith. People of all backgrounds, attracted by its unifying message, enter the Faith. While it spreads primarily by word of mouth, the Faith also grows due to the attention of notable, influential members of society.

1899

Olive Jackson, of New York City, becomes the first African American woman Bahá'í.

19 12

After a lifetime of imprisonment and persecution, 'Abdu'l-Bahá, the son of Bahá'u'lláh, travels from coast to coast across North America. Race unity is a theme of His many talks. He calls on America to become a land of spiritual distinction and leadership and gives a powerful vision of America's spiritual destiny—to lead the way in establishing the oneness of humanity.

'Abdu'l-Bahá as a young man

RACE IN AMERICA IN 1912

The country is torn with racial division, segregation and "separate but equal." 'Abdu'l-Bahá challenges Americans to go beyond tolerance, to embrace diversity, and to demolish racial barriers in law, education and marriage.

'Abdu'l-Bahá moreover has said,

"the colored people [can be likened] to the black pupil of the eye surrounded by the white. In this black pupil is seen the reflection of that which is before it, and through it the light of the spirit shineth forth."

APRIL 30, 1912

'Abdu'l-Bahá speaks at the 4th Annual Convention of the NAACP in Chicago. He was deeply admired by W.E.B. DuBois, and was featured in the May 1912 issue of the NAACP magazine, *The Crisis*.

1920s

Bahá'ís play a signifcant role in the South Carolina Gullah community in overcoming complex social, economic and political conditions to create a genuinely interracial religous community. The Bahá'í Faith later grows to be the second largest religion in the state.

NATIONAL SPIRITUAL ASSEMBLY OF THE BAHÁ'IS OF THE UNITED STATES ESTABLISHED

1925

"Temple Unity," established in 1909 to advance the construction of the Bahá'í House of Worship, was the precursor to the first National Spiritual Assembly of the Bahá'ís of the United States and Canada. (Photo from early 1940s)

1921

'Abdu'l-Bahá dies in Palestine. His Will and Testament names His grandson, Shoghi Effendi, to lead as Guardian of the Bahá'í Faith. He serves until his passing in 1957.

1912   **1916**   **1920**

ENCOURAGING INTERRACIAL MARRIAGE

Although 30 states enforce laws banning interracial marriage, 'Abdu'l-Bahá encourages it as a way to unite the races, saying that such marriages would produce strong and beautiful offspring.

'Abdu'l-Bahá encourages the marriage of Louis Gregory, an African American, and Louisa Mathew, a white English Bahá'í, in New York City. Their union serves as inspiration to generations of Bahá'ís who enter interracial and interfaith marriages.

Thou must endeavor that they intermarry. There is no greater means to bring about affection between the white and the black than the influence of the Word of God. Likewise marriage between these two races will wholly destroy and eradicate the root of enmity.

— 'ABDU'L-BAHÁ

MAY 1, 1912

Unusual for the times, women lead in getting the Bahá'í House of Worship built. Nettie Tobin provides the ceremonial cornerstone laid by 'Abdu'l-Bahá.

1916

'Abdu'l-Bahá issues "The Tablets of the Divine Plan," a collection of 14 letters written to North Americans emphasizing the need for them to share worldwide the unifying message of Bahá'u'lláh.

RACE AMITY CONFERENCES

1921

Bahá'ís in Washington, D.C., host the first of four Race Amity conferences held between 1921 and 1924, advancing the ideas of racial equality, harmony and amity. The goal is to unite the races at a time when gangs of white servicemen returning from WWI are attacking Black people.

In 1938, Shoghi Effendi, Guardian of the Bahá'í Faith, addressed a letter to the Bahá'ís in North America. Published in book form as *The Advent of Divine Justice,* this letter describes in clear and compelling language the gravity of the challenge to which Bahá'ís were being summoned and the vital importance of their actions in the establishment of the just, unified and peaceful world order envisaged by Bahá'u'lláh.

"Let the white make a supreme effort in their resolve to contribute their share to the solution of this problem, to abandon once for all their usually inherent and at times subconscious sense of superiority, to correct their tendency towards revealing a patronizing attitude towards the members of the other race, to persuade them through their intimate, spontaneous and informal association with them of the genuineness of their friendship and the sincerity of their intentions, and to master their impatience of any lack of responsiveness on the part of a people who have received, for so long a period, such grievous and slow-healing wounds. Let the Negroes, through a corresponding effort on their part, show by every means in their power the warmth of their response, their readiness to forget the past, and their ability to wipe out every trace of suspicion that may still linger in their hearts and minds. Let neither think that the solution of so vast a problem is a matter that exclusively concerns the other. Let neither think that such a problem can either easily or immediately be resolved. Let neither think that they can wait confidently for the solution of this problem until the initiative has been taken, and the favorable circumstances created, by agencies that stand outside the orbit of their Faith. Let neither think that anything short of genuine love, extreme patience, true humility, consummate tact, sound initiative, mature wisdom, and deliberate, persistent, and prayerful effort, can succeed in blotting out the stain which this patent evil has left on the fair name of their common country."

As to racial prejudice, the corrosion of which, for well-nigh a century, has bitten into the fiber, and attacked the whole social structure of American society, it should be regarded as constituting the most vital and challenging issue confronting the Bahá'í community.

— SHOGHI EFFENDI

1935
Bahá'í teachings begin to be systematically shared among members of the Oneida Nation and other American Indian populations.

40s-50s
Bahá'u'lláh's plan for Bahá'í institutions begins to take shape under the guidance of Shoghi Effendi. The Bahá'í community grows to encircle the globe.

New Deal Exclusion (1933 – 1964)

Mass expansion of convict leasing (1865 – 1941)

US Civil Rights Movement (1948 – 1968)

1935   **1940**   **1950**   **1960**

FHA Redlining (1934 – 1968)

Jim Crow, Black Codes, Pig Laws, & Separate But Equal (1877 – 1965)

SHOGHI EFFENDI GUIDES GLOBAL EXPANSION

1937
Shoghi Effendi issues the first of a series of plans that guide the systematic growth of the world-wide Bahá'í community.

1953
The Bahá'í House of Worship in Wilmette, Illinois, is completed. Dedication ceremonies draw more than five thousand people in an integrated gathering unusual for its time.

1963

The Universal House of Justice, the international governing council of the Bahá'í Faith, is first elected in Haifa, Israel. Amoz E. Gibson, an African American (with Creek Indian ancestry) from Washington D.C., is elected and serves until 1982.

1987

The Black Men's Gathering (BMG) is founded as a healing space for those suffering from a legacy of oppression. Annual summer gatherings run for 24 years and generate regional off-shoots and international service projects.

2017

The Bahá'í Office of Public Affairs begins a series of dialogues on Faith and Race and begins systematic efforts to contribute Bahá'í perspectives to the national discourse on race.

2016

The Bahá'í Chair for World Peace, an endowed research program at the University of Maryland, begins a multiyear effort to address structural racism.

1974

Bahá'í Youth Workshops reach young people battered by racism, gang violence and drug abuse. The workshops grow into a national expression of Bahá'í youth activity.

1980

The Native American Bahá'í Institute is founded. The campus is on 40 acres of piñon/juniper forest surrounded by the Navajo Nation.

1996

A framework for action is set in motion in the Bahá'í world to enable large numbers of people to study and apply spiritual principles to their lives and communities. In the quarter-century since, this framework has become the primary Bahá'í vehicle for personal and social transformation.

Racial injustice in law enforcement leads to a period of mass incarceration of African American men. (1971– present)

1970 **1980** **1990** **2000** **2010** **2020**

1963

The first Great Council Fire brings together Bahá'ís from more than two dozen native tribal groups nationwide to strengthen Indigenous peoples' contribution to the Faith.

1991

The National Spiritual Assembly of the Bahá'ís of the United States publishes "The Vision of Race Unity: America's Most Challenging Issue," a statement that is widely shared and discussed.

2011

The National Spiritual Assembly establishes a Social Action Desk to encourage the application of spiritual principles and capacities to social and economic development.

1985

The Universal House of Justice releases "The Promise of World Peace," a landmark statement in which it cites racial prejudice as one of the most significant impediments to world peace.

2002

The junior youth spiritual empowerment program is developed to foster the capacity for moral reasoning and a commitment to serving humanity among young people ages 12 to 14.

2019

"Walking Together on a Path Toward Race Amity" program begins at seasonal schools.

The diversity in the human family should be the cause of love and harmony, as it is in music where many different notes blend together in the making of a perfect chord.

— 'ABDU'L-BAHÁ

LEARN MORE AND

GET INVOLVED

The lack of social justice evident in our country today engenders a sense of urgency and determined focus. Millions long for the creation of a world in which knowledge will be the province of all; where there are no limitations imposed upon a soul by virtue of race, age, class, religion or gender; where the material and spiritual aspects of life are in harmony; and where all of the truths essential for human progress are held sacred.

To create such a world will require great sacrifice, courage and audacity. A rich tapestry of community life that increasingly reflects the beautiful diversity and unity of our human family will not emerge of its own accord. The evils of racism, materialism and moral decadence will be eradicated only by a love that is translated into action——such actions as deliberately going out of our way to befriend all, and sharing the efforts and contributions of all in the creation of a new world.

Ultimately, the power to transform the world is effected by love, love originating from the relationship with the divine, love ablaze among members of a community, love extended without restriction to every human being.

—THE UNIVERSAL HOUSE
   OF JUSTICE
   (INTERNATIONAL GOVERNING
   COUNCIL OF THE BAHÁ'Í FAITH)

Bahá'í House of Worship in Wilmette, Illinois

WALKING TOGETHER ON A
PATH OF SERVICE

The worldwide Bahá'í community is warm, vibrant, diverse and welcoming. We invite you to learn with us how Bahá'u'lláh's teachings are changing the world. We welcome people of all backgrounds to:

- Join a study circle (The first course is "Reflections on the Life of the Spirit." New groups are always forming.)
- Join a Bahá'í children's class
- Join a group exploring the junior youth spiritual empowerment program (for ages 12-14)
- Attend or host an informal devotional gathering
- Learn about Bahá'í service projects in your neighborhood

Start by contacting Bahá'ís in your local community. **Call 1-800-22-UNITE or go to** www.bahai.us/contact